Little People, BIG DREAMS
RUDOLF NUREYEV

Written by
Mª Isabel Sánchez Vegara

Illustrated by
Eleonora Arosio

Frances Lincoln
Children's Books

In the freezing north of Russia lived a little boy, named Rudolf. He preferred to spend hours alone inventing dance steps, than playing hockey with the rest of the children.

When he was seven, Rudolph went to the ballet with his parents and three sisters on New Year's Eve. Long before the theatre lights came on, he knew he would live for ballet.

His father thought that ballet was a 'girl thing'
and tried to change his mind. But Rudolf talked
of little else, and soon, he was enrolled in a class.

It was not until he was 17 that Rudolf found his way to a professional school. His teachers thought his style wasn't very tidy, but what he lacked in polish he made up for with intensity.

Rudolf would launch himself into fabulous pirouettes, lifting his body higher than any other dancer.

Soon, he became one of the leading figures
at the famous Kirov Ballet.

He didn't like the trunks that male dancers wore back then, and wanted to perform in tights, like ballerinas did. But many things were prohibited in Russia in those days, and Rudolf had to give up this demand if he wanted to keep dancing.

One day, Rudolf's company got permission to visit Paris.
When Rudolf finished his performance, he received
a standing ovation that lasted longer than the dance itself!
And then, there were movies, fancy shops, dinner parties...

He was not supposed to mingle with foreigners while he was in France. But Rudolf snuck off from the Russian secret agents who were watching him and just enjoyed himself.

On the day of his departure, Rudolf ran away from his guards and refused to get on the plane back home. He didn't want anyone to tell him how to dance, or who to love, anymore.

He was left with just a suitcase, but what he carried in his mind was much bigger: Rudolf introduced dancing techniques from the East into the best western companies.

Rudolph danced for years with the famous Margot Fonteyn, and showed the world that it doesn't matter who the danseur or ballerina is – great dancers simply deserve equal credit.

For almost 30 years, he kept electrifying
the world, bringing male dancing into the limelight,
and changing the course of ballet forever.

Little Rudolf showed the world that there are not 'things for girls' nor 'things for boys'. Only things that you love doing with your whole heart.

RUDOLF NUREYEV

(Born 1938 • Died 1993)

c. 1950s   1962

Rudolf Nureyev began his life in motion. He was born on a train, speeding across Siberia. He spent his early years in Irkutsk, Russia but his family had to leave when Germany invaded, and they moved to another town called Ufa, where they lived in poverty. The town was bitterly cold in the winter and Rudolf, a little boy of five years old, did not have any shoes. His mother carried him to school on her back. Although they lived in poverty, his mother managed to buy a single ticket to the ballet and sneak her children in. Rudolf was instantly captivated and asked his father for lessons. Unlike most future professional dancers, Rudolf only began his formal ballet training at age 17. He was not as good as everyone else, which sparked an intense work ethic that never left him. Rudolf was accepted into the Kirov ballet in 1958 and immediately started making a

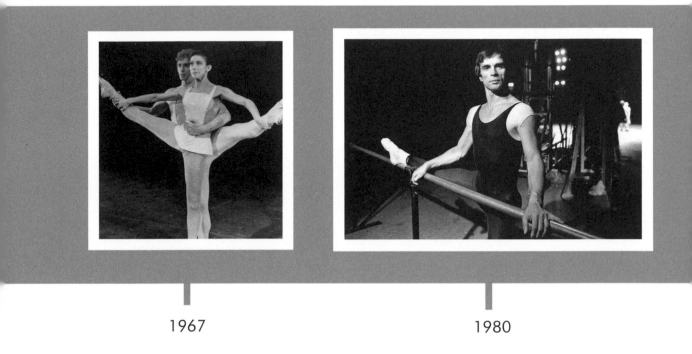

1967   1980

reputation for himself – both good and bad. He refused to dance in the
ballet shorts he was given, which he called 'lampshades' and insisted
that he should dance in tights like western dancers. Rudolf made a life-
changing decision on a trip to Paris, in 1961. He decided he would not
return to Russia. After that, Rudolf danced practically every role with every
company in the world, working with all the famous choreographers and
dancers, including the most famous ballerina of the moment: Margot
Fonteyn. Their partnership was electric. Rudolf's dancing was alluring
and energetic, and full of impressive jumps. Audiences loved them like
rock stars and people would wait in line for tickets. Rudolf also started to
choreograph and direct his own ballets, which cemented his status as a
legend. He is remembered as one of the greatest dancers in the world.

Want to find out more about **Rudolf Nureyev?**
Have a read of these great books:

Ballet: The Definitive Illustrated Story by DK

The Ballet Book by Darcey Bussell

If you're in London, you could visit the Royal Opera House, to see the stage
where Nureyev once danced.

BOARD BOOKS

COCO CHANEL

ISBN: 978-1-78603-246-1

MAYA ANGELOU
ISBN: 978-1-78603-250-8

FRIDA KAHLO
ISBN: 978-1-78603-248-5

AMELIA EARHART

ISBN: 978-1-78603-251-5

MARIE CURIE
ISBN: 978-1-78603-254-6

ADA LOVELACE

ISBN: 978-1-78603-260-7

ROSA PARKS
ISBN: 978-1-78603-264-5

EMMELINE PANKHURST

ISBN: 978-1-78603-262-1

AUDREY HEPBURN
ISBN: 978-1-78603-256-0

ELLA FITZGERALD

ISBN: 978-1-78603-258-4

BOX SETS

WOMEN IN ART

ISBN: 978-1-78603-403-8

WOMEN IN SCIENCE
ISBN: 978-1-78603-402-1

BOOKS & PAPER DOLLS

EMMELINE PANKHURST
ISBN: 978-1-78603-405-2

MARIE CURIE
ISBN: 978-1-78603-404-5

Collect the
Little People, **BIG DREAMS** series:

FRIDA KAHLO

ISBN: 978-1-84780-770-0

COCO CHANEL

ISBN: 978-1-84780-771-7

MAYA ANGELOU

ISBN: 978-1-84780-890-5

AMELIA EARHART

ISBN: 978-1-84780-885-1

AGATHA CHRISTIE

ISBN: 978-1-84780-959-9

MARIE CURIE
ISBN: 978-1-84780-961-2

ROSA PARKS
ISBN: 978-1-78603-017-7

AUDREY HEPBURN
ISBN: 978-1-78603-052-8

EMMELINE PANKHURST
ISBN: 978-1-78603-019-1

ELLA FITZGERALD
ISBN: 978-1-78603-086-3

ADA LOVELACE
ISBN: 978-1-78603-075-7

JANE AUSTEN
ISBN: 978-1-78603-119-8

GEORGIA O'KEEFFE
ISBN: 978-1-78603-121-1

HARRIET TUBMAN
ISBN: 978-1-78603-289-8

ANNE FRANK
ISBN: 978-1-78603-292-8

MOTHER TERESA
ISBN: 978-1-78603-290-4

JOSEPHINE BAKER
ISBN: 978-1-78603-291-1

L. M. MONTGOMERY
ISBN: 978-1-78603-295-9

JANE GOODALL
ISBN: 978-1-78603-294-2

SIMONE DE BEAUVOIR
ISBN: 978-1-78603-293-5

MUHAMMAD ALI

ISBN: 978-1-78603-733-6

STEPHEN HAWKING
ISBN: 978-1-78603-732-9

MARIA MONTESSORI
ISBN: 978-1-78603-753-4

VIVIENNE WESTWOOD
ISBN: 978-1-78603-756-5

MAHATMA GANDHI

ISBN: 978-1-78603-334-5

DAVID BOWIE

ISBN: 978-1-78603-334-5

WILMA RUDOLPH

ISBN: 978-1-78603-750-3

DOLLY PARTON

ISBN: 978-1-78603-759-6

BRUCE LEE
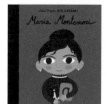
ISBN: 978-1-78603-335-2

RUDOLF NUREYEV

ISBN: 978-1-78603-336-9

Brimming with creative inspiration, how-to projects, and useful information to enrich your everyday life, Quarto Knows is a favourite destination for those pursuing their interests and passions. Visit our site and dig deeper with our books into your area of interest: Quarto Creates, Quarto Cooks, Quarto Homes, Quarto Lives, Quarto Drives, Quarto Explores, Quarto Gifts, or Quarto Kids.

Text © 2019 Mª Isabel Sánchez Vegara. Illustrations © 2019 Eleonora Arosio.

First Published in the UK in 2019 by Frances Lincoln Children's Books, an imprint of The Quarto Group.

The Old Brewery, 6 Blundell Street, London N7 9BH, United Kingdom.

T (0)20 7700 6700 F (0)20 7700 8066 **www.QuartoKnows.com**

First Published in Spain in 2019 under the title Pequeño & Grande Rudolf Nureyev

by Alba Editorial, s.l.u., Baixada de Sant Miquel, 1, 08002 Barcelona

www.albaeditorial.es

A catalogue record for this book is available from the British Library.

ISBN 978-1-78603-336-9

The illustrations were created in pencil and coloured digitally.

Set in Futura BT.

Published by Rachel Williams • Designed by Karissa Santos

Edited by Katy Flint • Production by Jenny Cundill

Manufactured in Guangdong, China CC052019

9 7 5 3 1 2 4 6 8

Photographic acknowledgements (pages 28-29, from left to right) 1. Young dancer Nureyev during exercise at the barre, c. 1950s © AGIP / Bridgeman Images 2. Rudolf Nureyev rehearsing in New York City, 1962 © Jack Mitchell via Getty Images 3. Rudolf Nureyev and Margot Fonteyn rehearsing at the Royal Opera House, London, 1967 © Central Press / Stringer via Getty Images 4. Rudolf Nureyev rehearsing at the London Coliseum, 1980 © Hulton Archive via Getty Images.

MIX
Paper from
responsible sources
FSC® C008047
FSC
www.fsc.org

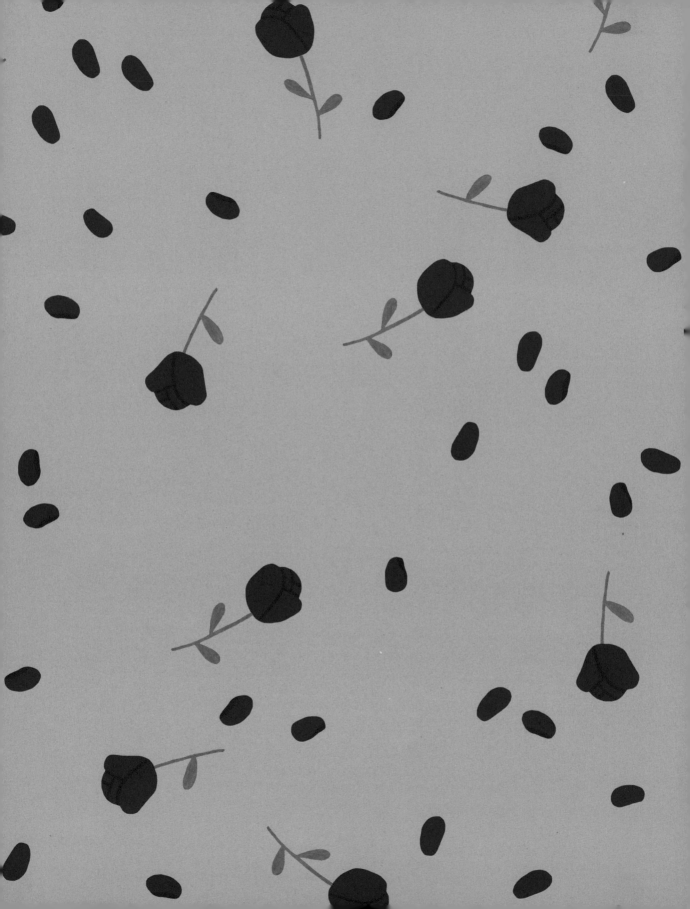